Just A Kindness

Written by Marsha Guerrier, Joshua Guerrier
Illustrations by Vladimir Cebu

This is a work of fiction. Names, characters, places and incidents either are the product of the author's imagination or are used fictitiously. Any resemblance to actual persons, living or dea, events, or locales is entirely coincidental.

Copyright © 2018 by Marsha Guerrier

All rights reserved. This book or any portion thereof may not be reproduced or used in any manner whatsoever without the express written permission of the publisher except for the use of brief quotations in a book review.

Published in the United States of America

First Printing February 2021

Illustrations by Vladimir Cebu, LL.B.
Cover by Shazeb1984

ISBN 978-0-9991297-3-9

Library of Congress 2021901808

Published by Women on the Rise NY, Inc.

Find us online at:
Visit www.hersuitespot.com

The book is Dedicated To
Grandma and Grandpa for teaching me kindness and all your love.

...just as I am!

It is raising your hand in class
when you have something to say...

...just as I do!

Kindness is forgiving someone...

...that made you feel unhappy
...just as I do!

Kindness is helping mom with chores around the house...

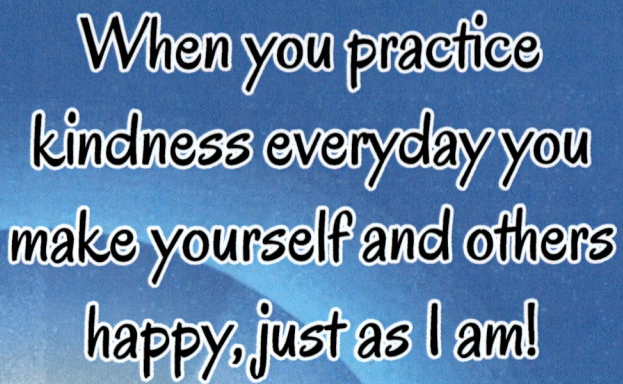

When you practice kindness everyday you make yourself and others happy, just as I am!

Made in the USA
Monee, IL
19 September 2022

13389553R00017